YOU CAN MAKE CHANGES

ASK OR IGNORE?

You Choose the Ending

by Connie Colwell Miller • illustrated by Victoria Assanelli

Do you ever wish you could change a story or choose a different ending?

IN THESE BOOKS, YOU CAN!

Read along and when you see this:

WHAT HAPPENS NEXT?

Skip to the page for that choice, and see what happens.

In this story, Yusra's neighborhood park has unsafe equipment. Will she ask for changes or will she ignore the problem? YOU make the choices!

It's a beautiful, sunny day in May. Yusra asks, "Dad, can I play at the park?"

Yusra's dad replies, "I'm sorry, but the park just isn't safe to play on. It needs to be torn down and rebuilt."

WHAT HAPPENS NEXT?

→ If Yusra asks what can be done, turn the page.
If Yusra goes to play inside, turn to page 20. ←

Yusra wants the park to be rebuilt. "How does a city park get torn down and fixed up?" she asks.

Dad replies, "Well, the mayor needs to know about the problem. That's the first step."

"Who should tell the mayor, Dad?" Yusra asks.

"Well," he says, "You could. You could write an email to her."

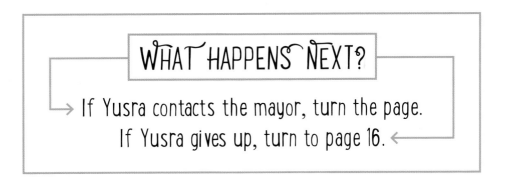

WHAT HAPPENS NEXT?

If Yusra contacts the mayor, turn the page.
If Yusra gives up, turn to page 16.

Yusra writes an email to the mayor, telling her how dangerous the park is. Her dad reads it over and they send it.

Yusra is worried. "Dad, what if the mayor doesn't write back? What else can we do?"

"We could talk to our neighbors and ask them to write emails, too," Dad says. But talking to people sounds difficult and a little scary to Yusra.

WHAT HAPPENS NEXT?

→ If Yusra and her dad go to talk to her neighbors, turn the page.

If Yusra waits for the mayor to write back, turn to page 14. ←

Dear Mayor Perez,
The park by my house is in bad shape. It is too dangerous to play on. Is there a way you could help us fix it so my friends and I have somewhere safe to play?

Sincerely,
Yusra

Yusra and her dad visit their neighbors. They ask them to call or email the mayor about the dangerous park. The neighbors start to spread the word to other people, too.

TURN THE PAGE →

After getting several emails and phone calls from Yusra and her neighbors, the mayor responds. She holds a community meeting to ask others about the park.

Everyone agrees it needs to be fixed up. The mayor begins to make plans for construction.

TURN THE PAGE →

The next month, a crew tears down the old park.
By August, Yusra's new neighborhood park is finished!

Yusra and the other neighborhood children can play there safely.

THE END

→ Go to page 23. ←

Yusra waits. The mayor is very busy, so she doesn't write back for several months. The mayor agrees to rebuild the park, but says it will have to wait until next summer.

Yusra is happy, but a year is a long time to wait for a new park. Maybe it would have been built sooner if she had told more people.

THE END

Go to page 23.

SUNSHINE

Discover the new
a place for gatheri
for all the family.

The four-acre park w
room' for our commu
the master plan, the p
flexible green space
picnic areas, access
tures, and a nature p

NEW PARK COMI

15

Yusra decides that telling the mayor isn't her problem. Someone else will probably do it. So she goes inside to watch TV.

TURN THE PAGE →

Weeks later, Yusra notices that no one has fixed the park yet.
Dad tells her, "People sometimes think solving problems is someone else's job. If everyone thinks that, then no one ever does the job."

Yusra should have told the mayor herself after all.

THE END

→ Go to page 23. ←

Yusra is disappointed. She wants to play at the park, but she figures nothing can be done. She plays inside with her dolls instead.

TURN THE PAGE →

Days and weeks go by and still no one fixes the park.
At summer's end, there is still no safe park where
Yusra and the other neighborhood children can play.

THE END

THINK AGAIN

- What choices did you make for Yusra?

- What happened? Did you like that ending?

- Go back to page 3. Read the story again and pick different choices. How did the story change?

Our choices have consequences, even when we don't act. If you noticed something needed to be done, would YOU do it, or would you leave it for someone else to do?

For Mrs. King's third grade class, especially Irene and Yusra.—C.C.M.

AMICUS ILLUSTRATED and AMICUS INK'
are published by Amicus
P.O. Box 1329, Mankato, MN 56002
www.amicuspublishing.us

Library of Congress Cataloging-in-Publication Data
Names: Miller. Connie Colwell. 1976- author. | Assanelli. Victoria. 1984-
    illustrator.
Title: You can make changes : ask or ignore? / by Connie Colwell Miller :
    illustrated by Victoria Assanelli.
Description: Mankato. MN : Amicus Ink. [2020] | Series: Making good choices
Identifiers: LCCN 2018053557 | ISBN 9781681516912 (hardcover) | ISBN
    9781681524771 (pbk.) | ISBN 9781681517735 (eBook)
Subjects: LCSH: Children--Political activity--Juvenile literature. |
    Community leadership--Juvenile literature. | Civic improvement--Juvenile
    literature. | Decision making in children--Juvenile literature. | Judgment
    in children--Juvenile literature.
Classification: LCC HQ784.P5 M55 2019 | DDC 320.083--dc23
LC record available at https://lccn.loc.gov/2018053557

Editor: Rebecca Glaser
Series Designer: Kathleen Petelinsek
Book Designer: Veronica Scott

Printed in the United States of America
HC 10 9 8 7 6 5 4 3 2 1
PB 10 9 8 7 6 5 4 3 2 1

ABOUT THE AUTHOR

Connie Colwell Miller is a writer, editor, and instructor who lives in Mankato, Minnesota, with her four children. She has written over 100 books for young children. She likes to tell stories to her kids to teach them important life lessons.

ABOUT THE ILLUSTRATOR

Victoria Assanelli was born during the autumn of 1984 in Buenos Aires, Argentina. She spent most of her childhood playing with her grandparents, reading books, and drawing doodles. She began working as an illustrator in 2007, and has illustrated several textbooks and storybooks since.